Ann Tompert
Charlotte & Charles
illustrated by John Wallner

Crown Publishers, Inc., New York

Also by Ann Tompert

Three Foolish Tales
Badger on His Own
Little Otter Remembers and Other Stories
Little Fox Goes to the End of the World

Text copyright © 1979 by Ann Tompert
Illustrations copyright © 1979 by John Wallner
All rights reserved. No part of this publication may be reproduced, stored in a
retrieval system, or transmitted, in any form or by any means, electronic,
mechanical, photocopying, recording, or otherwise, without prior written
permission of the publisher. Inquiries should be addressed to Crown Publishers,
Inc., One Park Avenue, New York, N.Y. 10016. Manufactured in the United
States of America. Published simultaneously in Canada by General Publishing
Company Limited.

10 9 8 7 6 5 4 3 2 1

The text of this book was set in 14 point Bookman Linotype.
The full-color illustrations were done in watercolors. The illustrations were then
camera separated and printed in four colors.

Library of Congress Cataloging in Publication Data
Tompert, Ann.   Charlotte and Charles.
Summary: Even though Charles insists that people always cause trouble for
giants, Charlotte wants people to visit their island. [1. Giants—Fiction]
I. Wallner, John C. II. Title.   PZ7.T598Ch   1979   [E]   78-26363
ISBN 0-517-53660-9

To Alex, many thanks

—J.W.

Two giants named Charlotte and Charles lived on an island in a château perched on the side of a mountain. Each day, when their chores were done, they would fly their kites or fish in the ocean. When nighttime came, they would walk hand in hand, studying the stars.

One day, while they were picking berries on the side of the mountain, Charlotte saw a fleet of ships sailing into the harbor.

"Visitors!" she cried. "Let's go down to the harbor and meet them!"

"I don't think we should, my dear. Sooner or later people always turn against us."

"We've been alone for so long," said Charlotte. "I would like to be with people again."

"I know," said Charles. "But we would be taking a chance."

"Please."

Charles sighed. "If it will make you happy," he said. "But promise me that you won't tell them our names."

"I won't," said Charlotte. "But things will be different this time. You'll see." And she ran home to get her favorite hat.

When she returned, the visitors were streaming down the gangplanks onto the shore.

"Do you think they'll like us?" she asked.

"We'll soon find out," said Charles.

When the visitors saw them, they fled in every direction.
Some hid behind rocks. Others pulled and shoved their animals
toward the woods. Some people dove into the water. But most
of them swarmed up the gangplank of the nearest ship and
huddled in a corner.

The ship began to tilt, and terrified screams filled the air.

Charlotte and Charles ran down to the harbor and leaned on the ship.

"Please don't be afraid," pleaded Charlotte. "We mean you no harm."

"Stay on our island as long as you wish," said Charles. "We will do everything we can to help you."

When the people saw how friendly they were, they decided to keep to their plan and settle on the island. And, true to their promise, Charlotte and Charles did everything they could to help them.

They graded roads with Charlotte's rolling pin. They built schools and shops wherever the settlers wanted them.

When the gardens needed rain, they squeezed water from the clouds. And on hot summer days they protected the village from the sun with their umbrellas.

In return for their help, the mayor presented Charlotte and Charles with a chest filled with gold and precious stones.

"We only want your friendship," said Charles.

"Yes," said Charlotte. "It means more to us than all the treasure in the world."

"Don't worry," said the mayor. "You will have our friendship until your dying day."

But during the following months, some of the settlers began to turn against Charlotte and Charles. "Someday they will use their strength to harm us," they said.

At first these settlers grumbled among themselves, but their suspicions soon spread throughout the island. Some people argued that Charlotte and Charles were too gentle to hurt anyone, but most grew to fear and resent them.

Nothing happened, however, until the settlers needed a bigger meetinghouse.

The settlers had gathered in the village square to decide what kind of building they wanted, and they could not agree. Finally the mayor said, "Maybe we could use something that is already built."

"Only the giants' château is big enough," said a carpenter.

"Let's take it away from them," said a blacksmith.

"We can't do that," said the mayor. "Not after all they have done for us."

A few people nodded in agreement, but they were too timid to say anything. Others voiced their fears and suspicions and demanded that Charlotte and Charles be driven from the island.

"Getting rid of them won't be easy," said the mayor. "It will take a clever plan. We will need the help of someone like Witt, the Wizard of Zug Island."

"Send for Witt! Send for Witt!" shouted the crowd.

One night, two weeks later, the mayor wrapped himself in a
cape and went to a deserted part of the island. He stood at the
edge of the water and peered out into the darkness. The moon
was covered with clouds, and all he could hear was the sound
of waves splashing against the shore. He swung his lantern
back and forth three times. Then he heard the faint sound of
oars in the water. The sound grew louder and louder. Then it
stopped. Two sailors appeared, pulling a boat onto the shore.
Witt stepped out of the boat and signaled to the sailors to leave.

"Thank you for coming," said the mayor.

"Did you bring the gold?" asked Witt.

The mayor handed him a leather pouch.

"Do you know the giants' names?" asked Witt.

"No," said the mayor.

"I thought not," said Witt. "Invite them to the village square tomorrow morning. I will meet you there."

Then he disappeared.

The next morning Charlotte and Charles arrived at the village square. A large crowd had gathered around two thrones. Witt was standing next to a table that held two crowns.

"Who is he?" whispered Charlotte.

"I don't know," said Charles. "But let's be careful."

The mayor stepped forward. "Since we owe all we have to you, we have decided to make you our king and queen."

Charlotte and Charles threw their arms around each other.

"You see," whispered Charlotte. "I told you that things would be different this time."

Charlotte picked up a crown. But as she put it on her husband's head, Witt said, "We need to know your names before we can crown you."

"Our names?" said Charlotte.

"He's a wizard," whispered Charles. "If he finds out our names, we will be in his power forever."

Charlotte stared at Witt. "We have no names we can give you. Why don't you make some up?"

"Come now," said Witt. "We must have your real names."

"Then we cannot be your king and queen," said Charlotte, and she took the crown from her husband's head and put it on the table.

Witt stroked his beard as he watched Charlotte and Charles climb up the mountain. "They are much more clever than I thought," he said.

"What will you try next?" asked the mayor.

"Bells," said Witt. "If giants hear bells, they turn to stone."

The next day, the village blacksmiths began to make a mold for an enormous bell. Carpenters measured the town square and cut lumber for a tower to hold it.

When Charles saw what they were doing, he began to pack a few of their favorite things in a knapsack.

"Let's wait a while," said Charlotte. "Maybe they will change their minds."

"What if they don't?" asked Charles.

Charlotte handed him a pair of earplugs that she had carved from a corkwood tree. "We will wear these whenever we go outside."

But the people did not change their
minds. They finished the tower and
began to ring the bell. They rang it day
and night, week after week.

Witt disguised himself and
followed Charlotte and Charles
everywhere they went,

watching and waiting
for them to turn to stone.

Then one morning the ground trembled beneath their feet, and a crack appeared in the roof of the château. Charles grabbed Charlotte by the hand, and they ran down the side of the mountain, jumped into the ocean, and swam away.

Witt ran down the other side of the mountain, shouting, "Stop the bell! Stop the bell!"

But it was too late. Trees fell. The earth cracked. Houses snapped in two and were turned upside down. People ran through the village looking for places to hide. The bell tower shuddered and fell to the ground.

Then everything was still. Not even a breeze whispered. The people came out of their hiding places and walked through the ruins. When they climbed up the mountain to the giants' château, all they found was Charlotte's hat.

"We have lost everything," said the mayor.

"We have lost our best friends," said a child who was sitting in Charlotte's hat.

Several years later, when Charlotte and Charles were studying the stars from the beach of their new island, Charlotte said, "It's lonely here with just the two of us. I wish some people would come to our island. We could make a village for them, and then..."

"And then," said Charles, "when they had everything they wanted, they would turn against us."

"Maybe they would," said Charlotte. "But the people would be different, and I would like to think that things could be different too."

THE UNPUBLISHED COLE PORTER

EDITED BY **Robert Kimball**

ARRANGEMENTS BY **George Terry**

MUSICAL SUPERVISION BY **Norman Monath**

SIMON AND SCHUSTER · NEW YORK

Music Autographing by Irwin Rabinowitz and Saul Honigman
Designed by Irving Perkins
Manufactured in the United States of America

1   2   3   4   5   6   7   8   9   10

Library of Congress Cataloging in Publication Data

Porter, Cole, 1891–1964.
    The unpublished Cole Porter.

    1. Songs, American.   I. Kimball, Robert.
II. Title.
M1629.P746S6   784'.0924   75–12730
ISBN 0–671–22093–4

Special thanks to John F. Wharton, attorney for Cole Porter and trustee of the Cole Porter Musical and Literary Property Trusts; to his assistant, Florence Leeds, for valued counsel and support; to Joan C. Daly, John Breglio and Philip Wattenberg for legal advice; to Cole Porter's family, friends and secretary, Madeline P. Smith, for preserving the unpublished Cole Porter songs; to Strome B. Lamon and Margaret Katz for editorial help in the preparation of this book.

To the memory of
Dick Simon,
who, some twenty-five years ago,
conceived and edited
The Cole Porter Song Book

—JOHN F. WHARTON
Trustee of the Cole Porter Musical
and Literary Property Trusts

Contents

Contents

Introduction

When Cole Porter died in 1964, he left behind him a large number of unpublished songs. Unlike most composers' "trunk music," they were not rejects, unresolved musical ideas or compositions below an acceptable musical mark: they in fact composed a body of work that would be the making of a lesser artist.

For Cole, like Irving Berlin and Sir Noël Coward, was not only a prolific composer but his own lyricist, and his "trunk music" was made up of completely finished songs. If a song did not work in a particular play or film, Cole was gifted enough to write one that did and wealthy enough not to have to worry about getting it placed elsewhere.

As a result, *The Unpublished Cole Porter* is a wonderfully rich collection of songs that today—more than 10 years after Porter's death and 17 years after he wrote his last song, "Wouldn't It Be Fun?," for the TV production of *Aladdin*—add immeasurably to the quantity and quality of his work already familiar to the public.

Born in Peru, Indiana, on June 9, 1891, the only child of Kate Cole and Samuel Fenwick Porter, Cole received his formal education and his musical training at Worcester Academy, Yale College, the Harvard Law and Music Schools and the Schola Cantorum in Paris. After an auspicious start as the composer-lyricist of the Yale football songs "Bulldog" and "Bingo Eli Yale," he suffered a professional setback when his first Broadway show, *See America First,* lasted for only 15 performances in the spring of 1916.

For much of the decade following World War I, Porter made Europe his home, especially Paris and Venice. Though disheartened by the failure of *See America First,* he continued to write songs, placing a few of them in English and American revues. In 1923 he wrote his first and apparently sole symphonic composition, the ballet score for *Within the Quota.* The ballet was a success in both Europe and the United States, but did little to spur Porter's ambition to write other extended works. For a time he took up painting, primarily as a hobby, while he continued to live the life of a playboy-expatriate member of international café society.

His marriage to Linda Lee Thomas in 1919 was the turning point in his life, and throughout their 35 years together (she died in 1954) she was his strongest supporter. Linda, a woman of taste and intelligence, had faith in Porter's talent, and she encouraged him to persevere in the face of indifference and his own lack of ambitious drive.

Porter did not have to compose for a living. In addition, he was a shy person, reluctant to fight for his own work. Even after he achieved success and was in demand as a writer for the musical stage, he was all too willing to accommodate some producer, director, author, performer or publisher who was dissatisfied with a song and wanted another in its place.

In October 1937, only a few years after he reached the top of his profession, Porter suffered a crippling horseback-riding accident. It left him in constant pain for the rest of his life and necessitated over 30 operations to preserve his legs from amputation. Yet in the midst of his personal agony he continued to create. Some of the best songs in this collection were composed after the accident that nearly cost him his life.

The songs in this volume represent only a small portion of the unpublished works of Cole Porter. I have tried to offer some pertinent information concerning the circumstances surrounding each song's composition and early history and some explanation as to why the songs were consigned to the trunk.

ROBERT KIMBALL

The Songs

"When the Summer Moon Comes 'Long"

The oldest surviving songs for which Porter wrote both words and music were composed during his freshman year at Yale (1909–1910). Manuscript copies of the two songs in Porter's hand were sent to his mother in Peru, Indiana. One, "Bridget" ("Bridget McGuire"), was published in the spring of 1910. The other, "When the Summer Moon Comes 'Long," was completely unknown until I found it by accident while examining a large scrapbook that Kate Porter kept of her son's college experiences. Hidden under some clippings in the scrapbook was an envelope that contained manuscripts of "Bridget McGuire" and "When the Summer Moon Comes 'Long."

"When the Summer Moon Comes 'Long"

Moderately slow and lightly rhythmical

Verse

1. If you want to wed a lit-tle girl, Sim-ply wild a-bout her,
2. When you've popp'd the ques-tion to her too, Af-ter you have kiss'd her, She'll

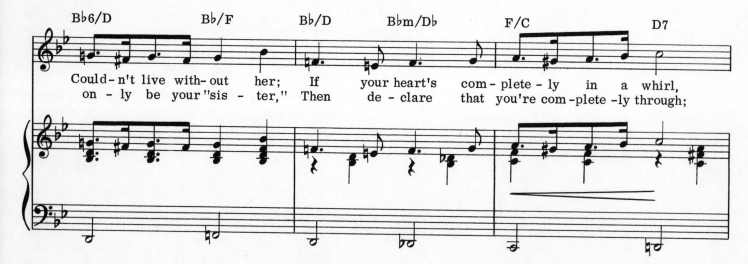

Could-n't live with-out her; If your heart's com-plete-ly in a whirl,
on-ly be your "sis-ter," Then de-clare that you're com-plete-ly through;

Just want to love__ and spoon;__ Don't pro-pose while win-ter-time is here.
Pad-dle her back__ home soon.__ Drift a-long un-til you've met a queen,

Wait till stars are gleam-ing, Wink-ing, blink-ing, beam-ing. Now's the time to
Some-one who will mar-ry, Won't put off or tar-ry. Take her to the

ask your lit-tle dear, Un-der the sum-mer moon.
spot where you've just been, Un-der the sum-mer moon.

Refrain

First se-lect__ a small ca-noe__ Where there's on-ly room for two.__

"Longing for Dear Old Broadway"

In 1954, author Almet F. Jenks, Jr., a member of the Yale class of 1914, presented Yale with four letters written to him by Porter during the summer of 1912. The letters concerned the collaboration between Porter and Jenks on a college musical entitled *The Pot of Gold,* for which Jenks wrote the book and Porter, the music and lyrics.

Included in Porter's letters to Jenks were some of the lyrics for the score of *The Pot of Gold*. The *Yale Library Gazette* had asked Porter's permission to use the lyrics contained in the letters to Jenks in a forthcoming issue of the publication. Porter replied in a letter dated December 7, 1954, "It will be perfectly all right for you to do whatever you wish with the lyrics of *The Pot of Gold*. Unfortunately, I have none of the music and none of the lyrics for this composition."

Porter was wrong, for scattered among the miscellaneous manuscripts that he bequeathed to Yale was virtually the entire score for *The Pot of Gold*. "Longing for Dear Old Broadway" is more than a bow to George M. Cohan's "Give My Regards to Broadway": it is both satire and tribute as well as an expression of Porter's own aspirations.

"Longing for Dear Old Broadway"

"The Tale of the Oyster"

Before Porter became an established composer for Broadway and Hollywood, he wrote many songs to amuse himself and entertain his friends.

One friend, the Princess San Faustino, the former Jane Campbell of New Jersey, was the leader of the international café-society set that thronged Venice's Lido during the summers of the 1920's. Each year Princess Jane, as she was known, provided a charity entertainment in which "scions of proud old Italian houses, members of the British nobility and daughters of American magnates combined in a jazz revue which for swing and pep would yield to no amateur show." Porter spoofed Princess Jane in a song which he originally titled "The Scampi." Outfitted with new lyrics and title, it became "The Tale of the Oyster" and was added to the 1929 musical *Fifty Million Frenchmen* during its Boston tryout.

When the production opened in New York in November 1929, critic Gilbert Seldes liked the show but lambasted "The Tale of the Oyster"—a very ingenious parody of a German lied—as a tasteless song about regurgitation. Although the song was admirably presented by comedienne Helen Broderick, it was dropped from *Frenchmen*, in deference to Seldes and the outraged expressions of others, shortly after the musical's New York opening.

"The Tale of the Oyster"

Down by the sea lived a lone-some oys-ter, Ev-'ry day get-ting sad-der and moist-er. He found his home life aw-f'lly wet And

longed to trav-el with the up-per set.___ Poor lit-tle oys-ter!

Fate was kind to that oys-ter, we know, When

one day the chef from the Park Ca-si-no Saw that oys-ter

ly-ing there And said, "I'll put___ you on my bill of fare."

"After All, I'm Only a Schoolgirl"

"After All, I'm Only a Schoolgirl" was introduced by Jessie Matthews in both the London and the New York productions of Charles B. Cochran's 1929 revue *Wake Up and Dream*. It is quite probable that the song was not published because its lyrics—witty as they are—were considered too risqué for their time.

teach - es me a lot, too: When to or - der a
ev - 'ry ex - hi - bi - tion, 'Cause he wants_ me to

ba - by car - riage And, bet - ter still, when not to.
stud - y Ve - nus In ev - 'ry known po - si - tion.

rall.

a tempo

Moderato, not too fast, and rhythmically
Refrain

Af - ter all,_____ I'm on - ly a school - girl,_____
Af - ter all,_____ I'm on - ly a school - girl,_____

What they call _____ an in - no - cent
What they call _____ an in - no - cent

"Why Don't We Try Staying Home?"

In 1929, New York's Mayor was James J. Walker, the handsome, high-living former lyric writer ("Will You Love Me in December as You Do in May?"). "Beau James" seldom missed a Broadway opening and during much of the decade, though married, openly courted an attractive chorus girl, Betty Compton. Under Mayor Walker's protective guidance, Miss Compton rose from the ranks of the chorus to play featured roles. Always willing to apply Walker's influence to make her wishes come true, she created many difficulties for *Fifty Million Frenchmen*.

When the show reached New York, she was so dissatisfied with her dressing room at the Lyric Theater that she complained to the Mayor, who slapped building-code violations on the theater and lifted them only when Miss Compton was given the star's dressing room, even though several other performers had superior claims to the room.

Similarly, Miss Compton wanted to snare the best songs in the score. She made a determined effort to wrest "You Do Something to Me" from the show's leading man, William Gaxton. When she failed, she made life difficult for Porter, who was compelled to write song after song for her in a valiant effort to satisfy her. "Why Don't We Try Staying Home?" is perhaps the best of the many songs Miss Compton refused to sing.

"Why Don't We Try Staying Home?"

Moderato, rhythmically

Verse

Since first we start-ed out,___ We've sim-ply run a-bout

Let us be-gin to cut___ The folks who mere-ly strut

And life's been one long rout___ un-end-ing.___

And talk of noth-ing but___ their in-comes.___

fast- er games___ fly by._____ Con- tent with
part- ies they're___ giv - ing._____ We're done with

be- ing slow,___ We'll nev - er let them know___
be- ing smart,___ And so we're goin' to start___

The nic- est place to go___ is bye- bye._____
To learn the gen-tle art___ of liv - ing._____

Refrain

Why don't we try stay - ing home?_____
Why don't we try stay - ing home?_____

41

"Pick Me Up and Lay Me Down"

In late 1931 Porter completed the score for his third consecutive musical for producer E. Ray Goetz. Like its two predecessors, *Fifty Million Frenchmen* (1929) and *The New Yorkers* (1930), the 1931 show *Star Dust* had a book by Herbert Fields. However, the show never went into production and very little is even known about it. According to Porter, the project collapsed when its principal backer, a large cigarette company, backed out after the government imposed an excise tax on cigarettes.

Porter's score for *Star Dust* included some of his best previously unused numbers, and three of the songs turned up a year later in *Gay Divorce*. Another song projected for *Star Dust* was "I Get a Kick out of You," later one of the hits of *Anything Goes* (1934) and a Porter masterpiece. Some of the songs written for *Star Dust* are lost or unknown, but among the survivors, "Pick Me Up and Lay Me Down" is outstanding.

"Pick Me Up and Lay Me Down"

Moderato, not too fast, rhythmically

Verse

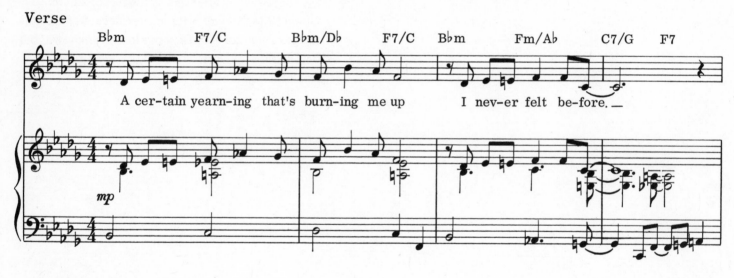

A cer-tain yearn-ing that's burn-ing me up I nev-er felt be-fore.

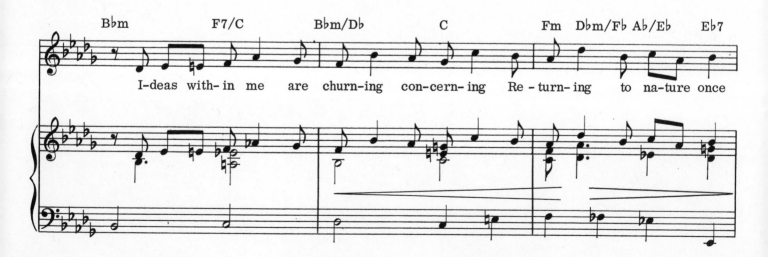

I-deas with-in me are churn-ing con-cern-ing Re-turn-ing to na-ture once

"When Your Troubles Have Started"

Red, Hot and Blue (1936) was anything but trouble-free. There were book problems, and a gargantuan battle over star billing between Ethel Merman and Jimmy Durante, although the third spot went uncontested to Bob Hope. There were even disputes between Porter and producer Vinton Freedley over the quality of Porter's score. The acrimony became so unpleasant for Porter that he did something uncharacteristic of him: he left the show—albeit temporarily—during its out-of-town tryout. The first act was apparently so lengthy that, according to Elinor Hughes of the Boston Herald, it was long enough for an evening of its own. Cuts of all kinds seemed mandatory, so out went a song from the opening scene, "When Your Troubles Have Started."

"When Your Troubles Have Started"

Moderato, not too fast

Delicately

Verse

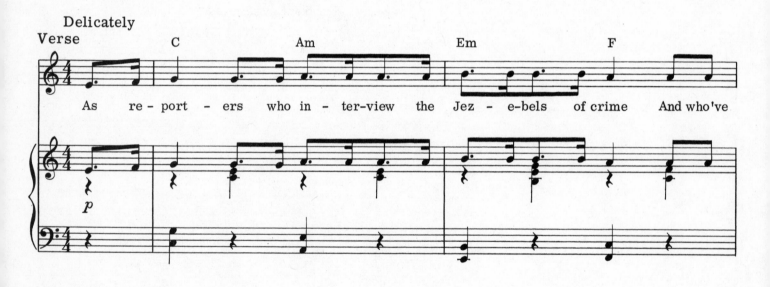

As re-port-ers who in-ter-view the Jez-e-bels of crime And who've

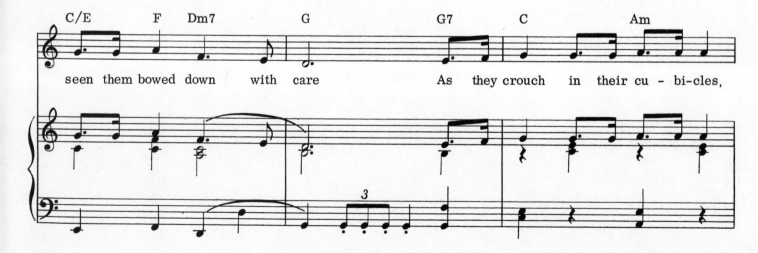

seen them bowed down with care As they crouch in their cu-bi-cles,

wait-ing for the time When they can feel the real com-fort of the chair, We have

grown so ac-cus-tomed to the trag - e-dies of life That if our

own lit-tle plans go wrong, 'Stead of ask-ing for ar-sen-ic or

call-ing for a knife, We sim-ply sing this song:

mot - to: "It might be a hell-uv-a lot worse."

1.
When your trou-bles have

To Patter
Slower
Tacet
For ex-am-ple, If your

3.
Fine

Patter
Moderato
phone is out of or - der, If your car is on the fritz, If you

sud-den-ly get the hic-cups When you're din-ing at the Ritz, If you

can't have ev'-ning call-ers 'cause your pa is such a prude, And he

can't pre-vent your moth-er from ap-pear-ing in the nude, If you

saw a dress at Saks for which you'd just give up the

ghost, Then you see it be-ing sport-ed by the

"I Know It's Not Meant for Me"

In the spring of 1937, Porter worked on the score for an MGM film, *Rosalie*, loosely based on the Broadway stage musical of 1928. The film starred Eleanor Powell, Nelson Eddy, Frank Morgan, Edna May Oliver, Ilona Massey, and a young singer-dancer named Ray Bolger. As this large, costly extravaganza became even larger and costlier, Bolger's part became smaller and smaller, and a song-and-dance number written for him, "I Know It's Not Meant for Me," was dropped from the film during production.

"I Know It's Not Meant for Me"

Slowly and gracefully

Verse

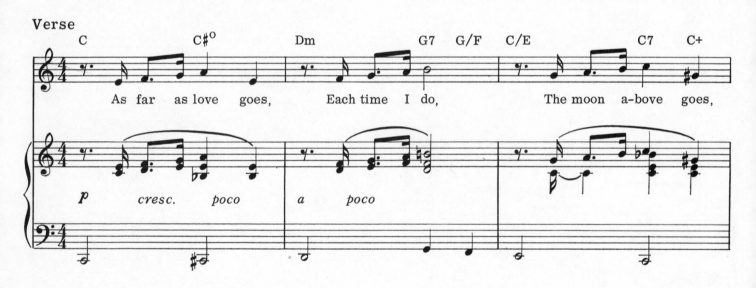

As far as love goes, Each time I do, The moon a-bove goes,

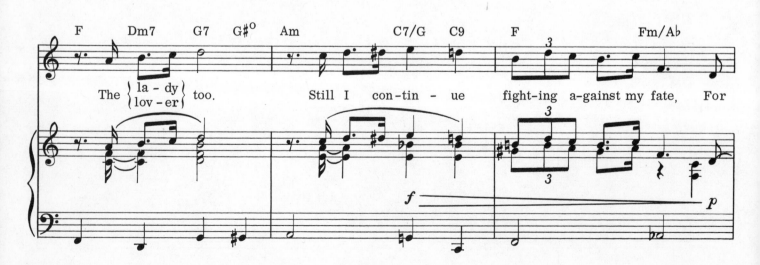

The {la - dy / lov - er} too. Still I con-tin - ue fight-ing a-gainst my fate, For

Oh, gee, it cer-tain-ly must be great-er than great To

Slowly with a flowing rhythm

Refrain

fall in love, to go in-sane, And then to find it was-n't

all in vain. What a joy that would be, But I

know it's not meant for me. To say, one day: "Per-

haps we might Be mar – ried soon," then, to your huge de-light, have your

sweet – heart a – gree, But I know it's not meant for

me. Nev – er daunt – ed ev – er schem – ing, What a

fool! Why am I al – ways dream – ing____ Of that home, sweet home I

"Greek to You"

"Greek to You" was the title song of an unproduced musical intended for presentation by Vinton Freedley in late 1937. The book was never finished, though, and the project was abandoned in 1938 with Porter having written only a few numbers.

"I'm Going In for Love"

In 1937 Porter suffered his crippling riding accident. In an effort to restore his sagging spirits, the Shubert brothers asked him to write the score for a musical version of the play *By Candlelight*. It was, in Porter's opinion, "the worst show I was ever associated with." Nevertheless, Porter retained a loyalty to the Shuberts, which he expressed by having his shows booked into Shubert houses as often as possible. As the ill-fated *You Never Know* staggered through a seven-month tryout in which the intimate drawing-room musical was transformed into a huge, typical Winter Garden production, several of its songs no longer seemed relevant to the ever-changing libretto—not that relevance was an especially sought-after quality in most musicals of the time. At any rate, Libby Holman sang "I'm Going In for Love" for a brief portion of *You Never Know*'s tryout.

"I'm Going In for Love"

I sup-pose all hus-bands are quite the same When it

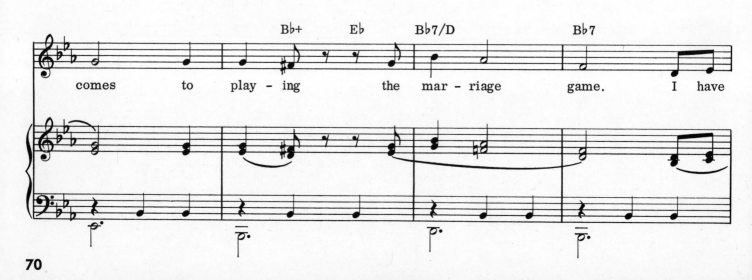

comes to play-ing the mar-riage game. I have

"I'm Throwing a Ball Tonight"

Since music publishers generally publish the songs they believe will become hits, it is not too surprising that this sparkling song, introduced by Ethel Merman in *Panama Hattie* (1940), was considered "special material." For though "I'm Throwing a Ball Tonight" is a song with tremendous musical drive and excitement, one is more struck, at first encounter, by its lyrics, with the topical references so typical of Porter.

"I'm Throwing a Ball Tonight"

Moderato

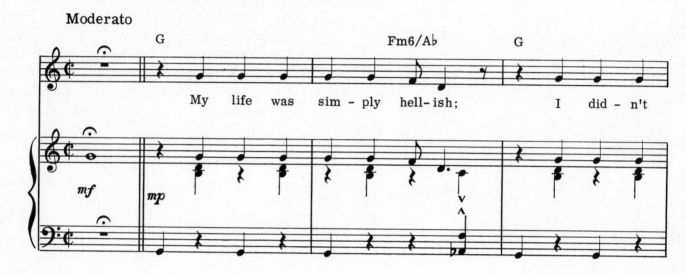

My life was sim - ply hell-ish; I did - n't

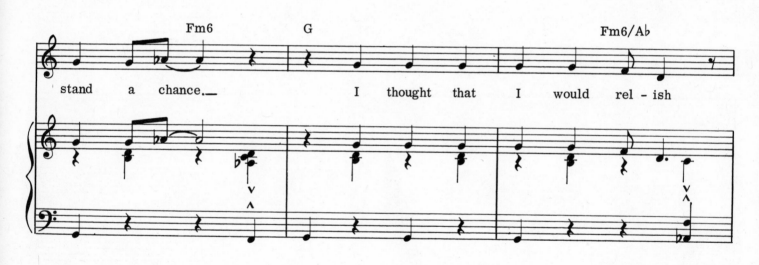

stand a chance.___ I thought that I would rel - ish

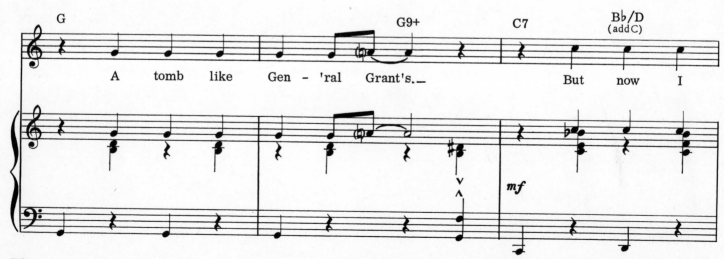

A tomb like Gen - 'ral Grant's.___ But now I

throw-ing a ball to-night.___ I'm full of the old pa-pri-

-ka; I'm load-ed with dy-na-mite,___ So

come on down,___ come on down,___ I'm throw-ing a ball to-night.___

___ A cer-tain per-son just brought some news___ And

vit – ed Mon – ty Wool – ley
vit – ed Gra – cie Al – len
vit – ed John – nie Walk – er,

And, of course, I asked Cliff O –
And, of course, I asked Fan – ny
And__ Haig and Haig I asked

dets.
Brice.
twice.

But to my sur – prise, Ev – 'ry one of those guys
But to all my bids Ev – 'ry one of those kids
But to my sur – prise, Ev – 'ry one of those guys

1. 2.
3.
To Tag

ten – dered his re – grets, And still I
wir – ed back, "No dice!" And still I
wir – ed back, "No dice!" And still I

Tag

feel like a mil – lion dol – lars; I feel sim – ply out of sight,__

So come on down,____ come on down,____ Come on down,____ come on down! I'm feel - ing____ mag - nif - ic;____ I'm throw - ing____ a tur - rif - fic ball _____ *(Shout:)* to-night!

"Mississippi Belle"
"I Like Pretty Things"
"When a Woman's in Love"

Throughout the spring and summer of 1943 and for a period in 1944, Porter worked on the score for *Mississippi Belle*, a film abandoned by Warner Brothers in 1944. As far as can be determined, Porter completed his work for the picture; it remains unclear why the film was never made. "Mississippi Belle," "I Like Pretty Things" and "When a Woman's in Love" were among the songs written for it.

Curiously enough, the same year that Warner's gave up on *Mississippi Belle*, the studio made use of a Porter song written ten years earlier for an unproduced Fox film, *Adiós Argentina*. It was a "trunk song," and its title was "Don't Fence Me In." It became one of Porter's biggests hits.

"Mississippi Belle"

Moderato, not too fast, and lightly rhythmical

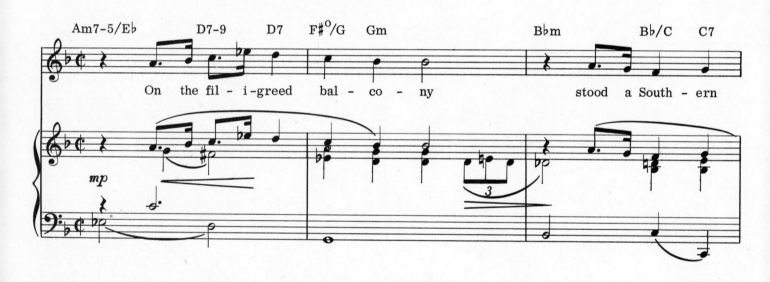

On the fil - i - greed bal - co - ny   stood a South - ern

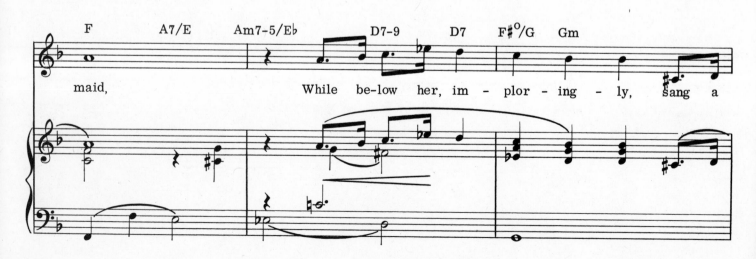

maid,   While be - low her, im - plor - ing - ly, sang a

Scent of jas-mine is heav - y____ And the fire - flies glow.____ Mis-sis-sip-pi belle,____ the night's en-thrall - ing____ And the mock-in'-bird's call - ing,____ "Come a-long, let's go!"____ 'Neath the mel-low moon,____ in all her

88

"I Like Pretty Things"

Moderato

Ad lib, not too slowly

Verse

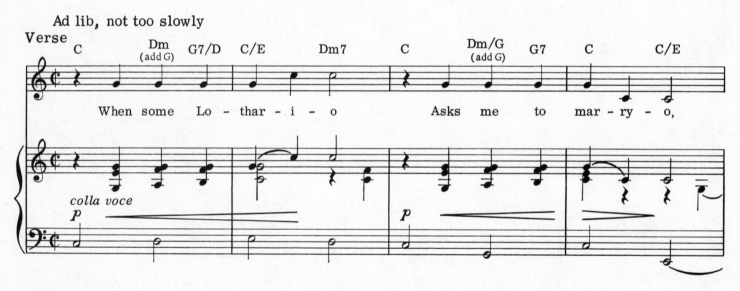

When some Lo - thar - i - o   Asks me to mar - ry - o,

I'm al - ways fair to him   And coy - ly de - clare to him,

"When a Woman's in Love"

Majestically

Moderato, rather lightly

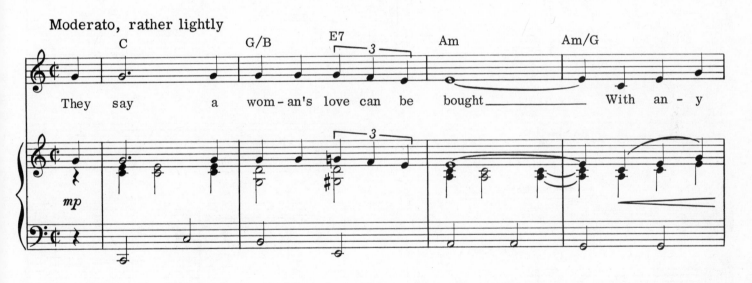

They say a wom-an's love can be bought_____ With an - y

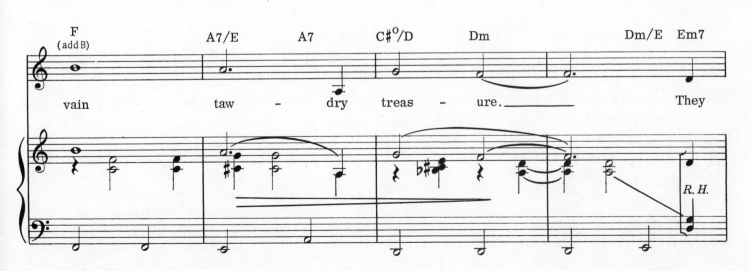

vain taw - dry treas - ure._____ They

say a wom-an's heart can be caught_____ By an-y in-
ane pass - ing pleas - ure._____ They
say, es - pe-cial-ly if she be fair,_____ That like a
bee the lea she rang - es,_____ Pur -

"It's Just Yours"

It is probable that "It's Just Yours" was written for Bobby Clark, star comic of *Mexican Hayride*, the Mike Todd extravaganza, with Porter songs, presented in 1944. But Clark either could not or would not sing the songs Porter wrote for him. As a result, approximately two of every three songs Porter wrote for this show were not used.

"It's Just Yours"

Moderately slow

Rubato and expressively

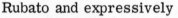

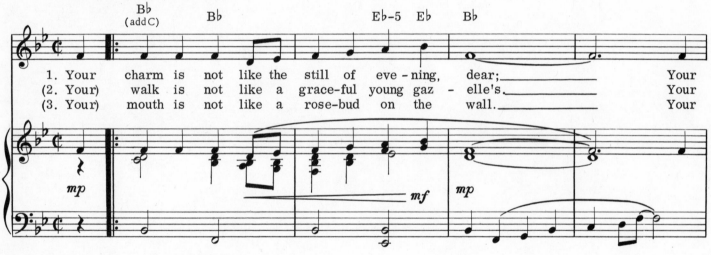

1. Your charm is not like the still of eve - ning, dear;_____ Your
(2. Your) walk is not like a grace-ful young gaz - elle's._____ Your
(3. Your) mouth is not like a rose-bud on the wall._____ Your

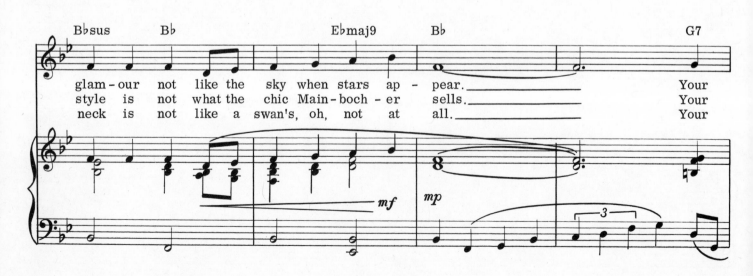

glam - our not like the sky when stars ap - pear._____ Your
style is not what the chic Main-boch - er sells._____ Your
neck is not like a swan's, oh, not at all._____ Your

"Manuela"

The Pirate was an MGM film released in 1948, starring Judy Garland and Gene Kelly. "Manuela" was a song obviously intended for Kelly, but it was cut from the film because it used rhymes on a girl's name, probably making it too similar to "Nina," also written for the film.

"Manuela"

cute as a kit-ten Who's got me so smit-ten, I've writ-ten a ser-e-nade. So here's _____ to my li-bi-do, _____ With a mi, mi, mi, re, re, re, mi do. Let's go! You're a

105

"I'm Afraid, Sweetheart, I Love You"
"Oh, It Must Be Fun"

When Porter was asked what was the most important development in the musical theater of the 1940's and 1950's, he unhesitatingly replied, "Rodgers and Hammerstein." What he meant was that after Rodgers and Hammerstein's *Oklahoma!*, *Carousel* and *South Pacific,* it would be very difficult to present a show in which the various elements (song, dance, story, etc.) were not closely coordinated, or "integrated." If a song was not specifically related to the book or the development of character in the story, it had to go out of the show no matter how strong it might be as an isolated song.

In the course of his work on *Kiss Me, Kate* (1948) and *Out of This World* (1950), Porter wrote several fine songs that were not closely enough connected to text or character development, so they were not used. "I'm Afraid, Sweetheart, I Love You" was dropped from *Kate* in the early stages of that show, while "Oh, It Must Be Fun" was cut in a similar fashion from *Out of This World*.

"'I'm Afraid, Sweetheart, I Love You"

Slow Beguine

I'm a-fraid,_____ sweet-heart, I love you;_____

I'm a-fraid _____ that's what is wrong._____

"Oh, It Must Be Fun"

Moderato, not too slowly

Verse

Ev - 'ry girl I know_____ Has her

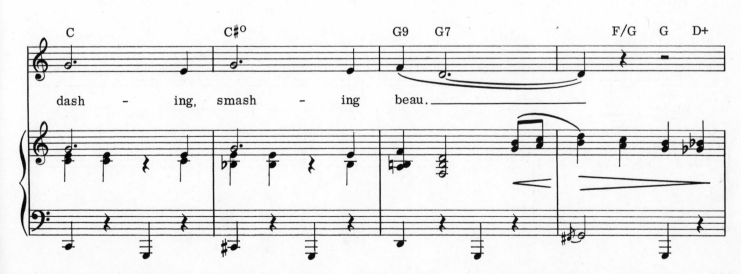

dash - ing, smash - ing beau._____

Ev - 'ry girl but me _____ Has her

build - er - up - pa cup - pa tea. _____

Ev - 'ry oth - er quail _____ Has her

trail - ing, wail - ing male, _____ So I

There - fore I re - peat, Oh, it must be sweet

To turn on the heat With the one you love,

1. With the one you love.

2. With the one_____ you

love._____

"To Think That This Could Happen to Me"

"Who Said Gay Paree?"

"When Love Comes to Call"

After *Out of This World* closed in May 1951, Porter began work on the show that became *Can-Can* (1953). When Porter wrote "To Think That This Could Happen to Me," he sent it to his collaborator, author-director Abe Burrows. Burrows reacted by telling Porter that he wanted a song that would be a more dramatic statement, revealing more about the character of the leading man at a specific point in the book. Once again, the requirements of the story forced the elimination of a song, and "I Am in Love" replaced "To Think That This Could Happen to Me."

The difference between "Who Said Gay Paree?" and "I Love Paris" is the difference between a song of bittersweet sadness and one of jubilant affirmation. It is hard to know why there was not room in *Can-Can* for both songs, but the wider range and greater rhythmic complexity of "Who Said Gay Paree?" may have posed too many vocal problems.

Similarly, the reason "When Love Comes to Call" gave way to "C'est Magnifique" (with its range of barely an octave) may also have been the stars' vocal limitations. While "C'est Magnifique"—more Gallic in spirit—is a song of considerable charm, "When Love Comes to Call" seems of greater power and richness in almost every way.

"To Think That This Could Happen to Me"

Moderately slow Beguine

"Who Said Gay Paree?"

Moderately slow and smoothly

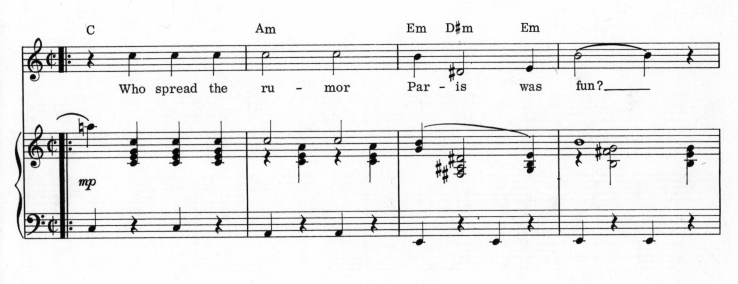

Who spread the ru – mor Par – is was fun?____

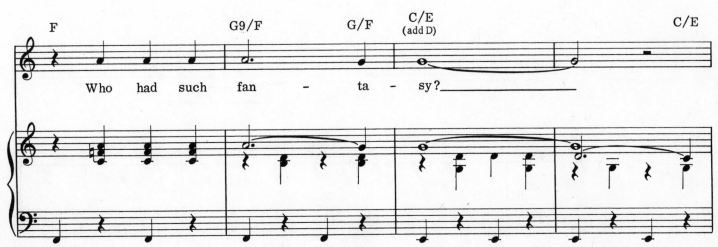

Who had such fan – ta – sy?_____

"When Love Comes to Call"

Moderato, smoothly

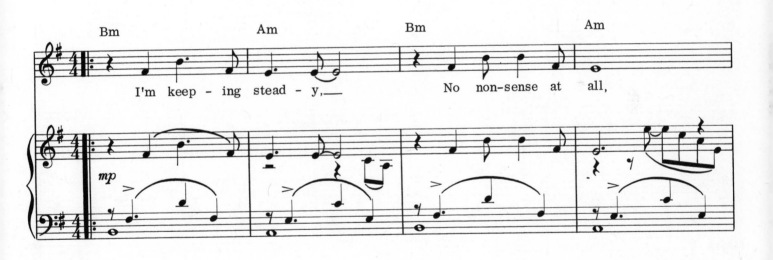

I'm keep - ing stead - y,___ No non-sense at all,

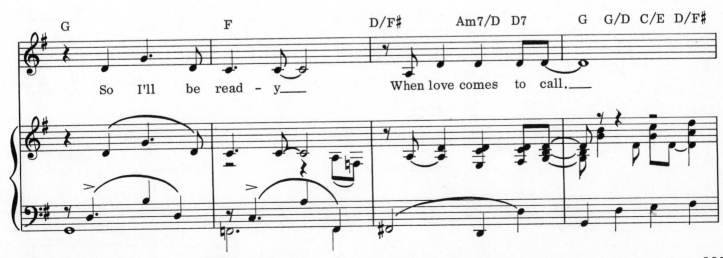

So I'll be read - y___ When love comes to call.___

"Give Me the Land"

This song was written for *Silk Stockings* (1955), which turned out to be Porter's last Broadway show. It is possible that some people felt the lyric was too pointed in its barbs at American life in the mid-fifties. It is also likely that the script called for a song better tailored to the character of the dumb Hollywood star. Indeed, "Stereophonic Sound," memorably presented by Gretchen Wyler, is hardly a song one would want to dispense with. Nevertheless, "Give Me the Land," a humorous parody of "God Bless America," is equally amusing and showed that right to the end of his career, Porter still had his incomparable wit and zest.

"Give Me the Land"

Sprightly

Verse

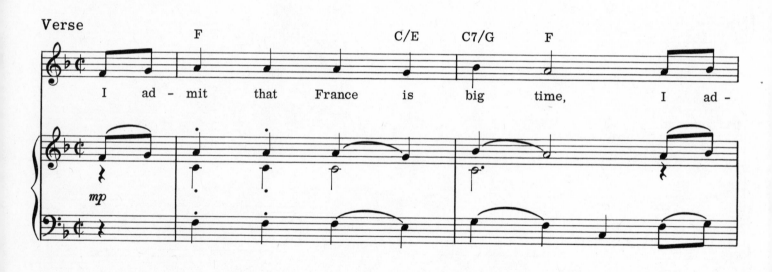

I ad – mit that France is big time, I ad –

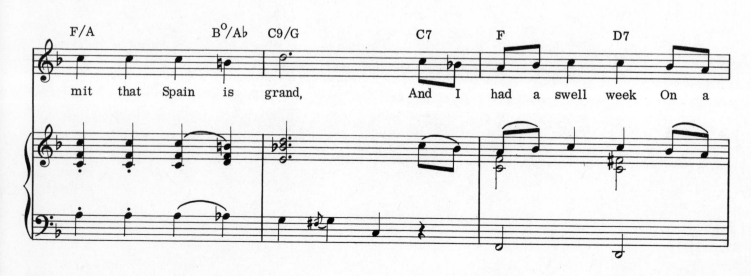

mit that Spain is grand, And I had a swell week On a

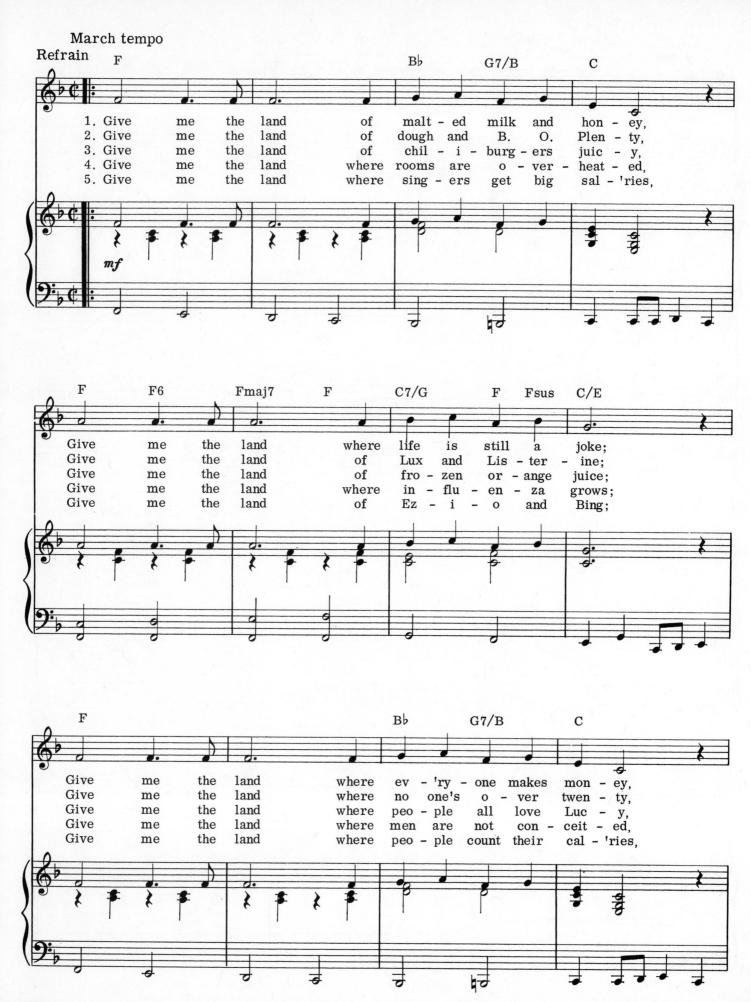

Give me the land where ev-'ry-thing's o-kay.

1. – 4.

Give me my pet coun-try, Give me the U. S. A.
Give me pub-li-ci-ty, Give me the U. S. A.
Give me a-ci-di-ty, Give me the U. S. A.
Give me de-lin-quen-cy, Give me the U. S. A.
Give me Va-ri-e-ty,

5.

Give me the U. S. A.

"High-Flyin' Wings on My Shoes"

"High-Flyin' Wings on My Shoes" was dropped from the film *Les Girls* (1957) when director George Cukor wanted to subordinate the score to the script. Had it been retained in the film, "High-Flyin' Wings" would have been sung and danced by Gene Kelly.

"High-Flyin' Wings on My Shoes"

Index of Song Titles

Index of First Lines